DIRTY WORK

To Heather
with all my love

Baku
19th January 2004

DIRTY WORK

ANGELA KIRBY

[signature]

Shoestring Press

Typeset and printed by Q3 Print Project Management Ltd,
Loughborough, Leics
(01509) 213456

Published by Shoestring Press
19 Devonshire Avenue, Beeston, Nottingham, NG9 1BS
(0115) 925 1827
www.shoestringpress.co.uk

First published 2008
© Copyright: Angela Kirby
The moral right of the author has been asserted.
ISBN: 987 1 904886 83 9

Shoestring Press gratefully acknowledges financial assistance from
Arts Council England

For my children, grandchildren and
Mike, with love.

ACKNOWLEDGEMENTS

Acknowledgements are due to the following, where many of these poems first appeared *Ambit, Artemis Poetry, A Twist of Malice, Images of Women, How Have I Loved Thee, In the Company of Poets, Magma, Mslexia, No Holds Barred, Peterloo, Resurgence, Rialto, Succour, Speaking English, The Shuffle*
also Radio Romania Cultural

I would like to thank Peter Abbs, Anne-Marie Fyfe, Christopher Reid, Maurice Riordan, Matthew Sweeney, Greta Stoddart and, in particular, Roddy Lumsden, for their inspirational help, criticism and support.

CONTENTS

TRIZONIA

O most excellent donkey who,
not having heard of the sleep button,
woke me three times this morning
with your ancient and execrable lament,
do you bemoan the start
of your overburdened day
and the end of your brief night's rest
in this unpromising patch of scrub
or do you, perhaps, grieve for me
who today must leave this incomparable islet
where there are neither cars
nor motorcycles, where nothing
very much happens, apart
from the occasional birth or marriage
and the rather more frequent deaths,
where there is little to see, just Iannis
repainting the peeling mermaid
on his taverna, and his grandmother
taking a broom to the six hollow-ribbed cats
who have stolen yet another chicken-leg,
and the three old men who,
having finished their backgammon
and the last of the ouzo, now take
the sun's path home across the harbour
in a boat as blue as that clump of scabious
you are considering?

I WANT TO TELL HER

I want to tell her,
the woman opposite me,
look, loosen up a little,
don't let on, don't
let them see, nobody
loves a loser – because
it's too old for her,
that drawn and weary face,
that turned-down mouth,
those seen-it-all eyes –
but now she leans forward
and I see her breasts
and they are beautiful –
and I want to tell her, look,
men will always love you
for your beautiful breasts
and, with a bit of luck,
one of them, one day,
will take your face
between his hands, and
with a bit of luck, will kiss
your down-turned mouth
back into laughter.

JULIA'S DOVES
i.m Julia Casterton

we reach the long-planned
rendezvous and find you gone

we search for your doves
but they are nowhere to be seen

there is only the grief of gulls
the scent of pine, the hot sun

and white-fingered waves
clawing at the rocks below

instead of a wreath
we pick these flowers

the small wild flowers
of Finisterre

yellow bell-flowers, gentians
wild thyme, white campion

and cast them out to sea, watch
as the wind lifts and scatters them

towards the Atlantic horizon
like birds, like butterflies, like words

.

FINAL REDUCTIONS AT THE SOFA WORKSHOP

He changes things slowly, one by one,
a feeling of disloyalty each time –

a new kettle when the old one blows,
a blue enamel egg-pan to replace

the one she burned dry, time and again,
a single bed, room now for a desk

where he can lay out his stamps –
she would never have allowed that –

his niece buys him a gramophone,
he plays his 78s: Gershwin, Berlin,

Rodgers and Hammerstein, Cole
Porter, smoke gets in his eyes,

she was the cream in his coffee,
she was the salt in his stew.

You could do with a new sofa,
his niece says, frowning at the stain,

and a chair while you're about it,
there's a sale on till Saturday.

Sofa, so good says the sign –
but he doesn't get the joke,

carefully, he sits in every one,
makes sure he can get up again,

two hours later he has settled
on cherry-red linen, pleased

with the brightness – his niece
doubts it is really suitable –

This is our Miranda range, Sir,
the salesgirl says, *a very good choice* –

she smiles at him, leans
forward to present the bill –

and free delivery – her blouse gapes,
breasts overflow the bra's half-shells,

he stares, cannot help himself,
he longs, longs to touch them,

the niece tugs him to his feet,
buttons him into his coat.

FATHER SHAUGHNESSEY

Together we are studying
The Mystical Body of Christ, all of us,
not least Father Shaughnessey,
floundering. There is ink
on the coconut-matting, the sun
beatifies him with dust and we
reluctantly-fasting
Children of Mary
are making a meal of him,
poor red-faced, red-haired boy,
fresh out of Maynooth
and way out of his depth.

His Adam's-apple, a stomper,
breaks into a jig, he grows
cack-handed, drops the encyclical,
flushes, sweats but, still game,
lips moving in silent prayer,
laces string to-and-fro
across the classroom
in a doomed attempt to illustrate
Christ's place within the Cosmos
which baffles us and leaves him caught,
close to tears, struggling
at the centre of the web.

Oh, Father Shaughnessey, we love you,
we are aghast, we mourn, repent,
unwrap you tenderly.

AILANTHUS

They have cut down the Tree of Heaven
which, until yesterday, grew tall
in the garden opposite my house
and my neighbours have done this
and even though it was very large
and stood by their front windows
and must have taken some of their light
it is hard for me to forgive them
for it had noble, deep-ribbed bark
and long fern-like leaves
and every summer it bore racemes
of delicate white pea-flowers
and the birds flew in and out
and in winter they clustered
like souls on the bare branches
and the blackbird continued to sing
of love from the topmost twigs
and now I can find little solace
in the short bare trunk that remains.

BEECH HILL
for I.M.Birtwistle, 1918 –2006

Last night the loon flew over from Long Pond
to Echo Lake – and onwards, far beyond

our darkening woods, mourning as she went –
now, after these six long hot hours, hard spent

in hacking out a path down to the shore
I take the Beech Hill road, past Charlie's door

then on by Sunset Farm towards Beech Cliff
to hear her call again, but nearer still, as if

to join, in counterpoint, the coyote's wild grief
with mine – that you're not here. I watch the brief

trajectories of passing satellites
between the falling stars, see, as the lights

of Todd's old pick-up brush across the lawn,
the soft and startled eyes of doe and fawn.

DAVY GRAHAM AT NICK'S DINER, 1964

Here's my baby, dressed in white,
if your love's for me, won't you stay the night?

One a.m. in Ifield Road,
Chelsea's paving-stones
are hanging on to the heat,
the Diner's hopping,
a solipsistic bubble
on the point of implosion,
but Serafina's there,
and she's cooling it.

Why's my baby dressed in black?
well now baby, won't you please come back?

Tonight he starts with Gary Davis –
in the kitchen the mayonnaise
curdles, Italian Joe sweats,
making his nightly grab for Sasha
as she collects two Steaks Tartare
and four Oeufes Florentine
for Table Six – as usual,
she knees him.

Oh baby, baby, please come quick,
this old Cocaine's making me sick –

The new waiter, an Adam Faith
look-alike, tips a bottle of wine
over Reggie Kray and a merchant
banker - there's a hush, Nick hovers,
charms, smoothes things –

Davy leans over the guitar,
long legs akimbo, candlelight
lurking in his hair.

Here's my baby, dressed in blue,
well now, lover, what's the matter with you?

At the till, Sasha sulks,
for now, having given them
a sweet How Long Blues,
wandered his way
through Muddy Waters, Bach,
Art Blakey and Big Bill Broonzy,
he is finishing off with *Anji* –
which she hates.

Tomorrow he'll move on,
to Bunji's or the Troubadour,
play them folk, blues – and maybe
something else, something
that is far, far beyond.

SINGLES NIGHT AT THE MADRUGADA

All right, all right, if you insist – third turn on the left into Deadpan Alley, any time after midnight, knock twice, whistle the first three bars of, say, the second track on The Return of Dr. Octagon, and Rat-Butt Billy will let you in if he likes the tune and the look of you - don't try too hard, he's got a nose for the prick, the prat, the poseur and the ponce – just take things easy, a nod's OK, but for God's sake don't smile – Billy has this thing about guys who smile – his wife dumped him for the drummer from Hot Black Stardust, the thin one, with the sea-snake tattoos, who's had his teeth fixed – and watch out for the strobes, they may reveal more than you'd care for, hard to describe – let's put it this way, I've seen sights in there that are best forgotten, so don't say I didn't warn you – one more thing – you can trust Chitty Moll, Bang-Bang and the Siamese twins but if a baby-faced tranny turns up in a silver shift and high-heeled sneakers, and offers you a white rose, get out of there fast, I mean fast and don't look back – believe me.

DIRTY WORK

They have been here before us,
those other ones,
leaving a resonance in the air,
a bloom of fingermarks
on the furniture,
burns on the fumed oak.

Did they too put their cases down
side by side on the thin carpet,
lock the door, blow dust and hair
from the bedside table,
think the stain on the ceiling
looked like Australia?

You unwrap champagne,
I open caviar, we share one spoon,
it takes more than a hard bed
and a dim lamp to deter us
but the bottle looks awkward here,
like gentry at a village wedding.

When the last bubbles burst
we stand hand in hand
at the window. Look, you say
even the glass is dirty
and you breathe on it,
tracing the usual patterns,
twined initials, arrows, hearts.

A FIRM PURPOSE OF AMENDMENT

Thirty years since my last Confession,
Father, but it's never too late, is it?
and what with one thing and another,
the letters from the clinic and that,
I thought well, can't do any harm,
might even do some good – still,
after all this time, believe me, Father,
it's not easy, though back when I went
regular, every other Saturday,
it only took me a minute
to say the lot – and all I'd get
was a couple of Hail Marys
which just shows you – well,
we were brought up to be pure, see,
and I was – for ever so long
but things change, Father,
you'll have found that
and if you want to know the truth
purity didn't get me anywhere –
there wasn't a lot of call for purity
round our way – so in the end
I gave it up and now look at me,
I could rattle on in here for hours
though with things that
to be honest with you, Father,
it's difficult to tell a priest
but then they do say, don't they,
you can't tell the Jesuits anything
they haven't done themselves –
oh, don't mind me, Father,
it'll be the Protestants as put
that one about – now, where was I?
Bless me, Father, for I have sinned
or should that bit have come first?
it's funny what you forget.

ROMAN HOLIDAY

Map-reading, I missed a turning
and sent us off down that wrong track

from which it took more than the half-hour,
three tolls and a fistful of lire to get back.

By the time we stopped in Sirmione
the car had overheated and the atmosphere

was dire. Not that you shouted, I'll say that
for you, but your self-restraint was sour.

Next day I was all set to walk out, but –
you pull the same tricks every time

and, forever the patsy, I fall for them –
when your fingers slowly climb

that indignant ladder of my spine
or stroke those last three vertebrae,

when you laugh, kiss my eyelids, quote
Catullus, his *da mi basia mille* – I stay.

GRAFFITI

Woken at midnight, I follow arrows,
like a childhood game, toward Casualty
and find you here in this bleak cubicle.

Sixteen, still in your party gear, all black –
stockings, shirt and scarf, your
grandmother's jet beads, a tattered shadow
sprawled against these cracked white tiles
where someone has sprayed
Fuck the Bastards.

I stretch out a hand to touch you, lift
the hair back from your smeared cheeks,
back from the vomit-crusted O
of your mouth, but you push me away,
and these black tears, scrawled
across the whiteness of your face,
are the only message you have for me.

PORTRAIT OF MISS FREDA MARWOOD
(taken in the Amy Sharples Studio, Blackburn, 1919)

To her father's exasperation
she wears the sort of clothes

favoured by Miss Sackville-West –
a type of woman he has no time for –

beneath a wide-brimmed felt hat,
she turns towards me an enigmatic

half-profile above her softly-tailored shirt,
loose tie, goose-winged breeches,

buttoned gaiters, those neat
well-polished boots – a woman

caught by the throat, choking
in the closeness of gas-lit rooms,

endless croquet summers
and charades of winter, stuck there

with a blithely selfish father, three
shell-shocked brothers and an ailing

sister, stuck here in this family album,
time-warped in that long denial.

UNLACING MY MOTHER

You don't need a corset, we protest,
exhausted, struggling at midnight

to untie the knots she's made
with her blind, swollen-jointed

fingers in the tangled strings –
as always, she replies, *but darlings,*

it's so comforting – she sighs,
and clasps her hands defensively

across her breasts, while behind her,
we roll eyes together. It seems

to take an age before she's freed,
swapping whalebone and pink satin

for a flower-sprigged nightdress.
We smooth sheets, rearrange pillows,

settle her in – and then lean forward to
receive her kisses, her *God bless*

and those same thumb-traced crosses
made upon our foreheads every night

when we were children. Now we, in turn,
dim the lights and leave her door ajar.

THRELKELD'S BULL

At the beginning it is the tulip curtains, the light pouring through
them, the dustfish rising and falling in the light, and the halo of
the mother's hair as she leans over the child's cot

or perhaps the beginning is in the pram under the apple-trees, the
shifting of green and gold overhead, the brief warmth of the wet
flannel-sheet beneath the child, the whistling of Harold, the milk-
boy, as he climbs over the stile

and either way, next it is *Holy Holy Holy*, with the father holding
the child to his shoulder, *Lord God Almighty*, sings the father,
beating the child's back softly, heels rocking on the nursery floor,
flames flicker-flack behind the brass-trimmed fireguard

then Hilda and Mollie are singing in the kitchen, *Moonatsy,
shining so bright, guide my lover tonight, Moonatsy*, they sing, for
they are walking-out with Peadar and Danny, over for the
haymaking, and the child watches as each man drinks a half-
gallon of cold tea, straight from the can, their cheeks cherry-bright,
but Martha Thorpe says that is TB roses

later still, in the lower meadow, red-white-and-blue bunting flitters
between the elm trees, *God Save Our Noble King* sing the
schoolchildren, and bob-haired, black-stockinged girls skip over
the twisting ropes, *one-pertater, two-pertater, three-pertater four –*

and Amos Fazackerley wins the Sack, Enoch Fazackerkey wins the
Egg-and-Spoon, together they win the Three-legged, which isn't
fair, and the child cries when her sister drops her near the end of
the Wheelbarrow-race, sure she should have won –

Mr Povey-the-vicar says a prayer for the Prince of Wales, Lady-
Mardy-from-the-Hall gives out prizes, poor old Batty-Patty, whose
love died in the trenches, runs here, there and everywhere, while
Miss Gornall-from-the-school pours out fresh lemonade into green
crackle-glass tumblers and rations the children to one each –

soon after that it is bedtime, a tin-bath by the fire, warm towels, hot milk, iced biscuits, and *eeh, that Mrs. Simpson,* says Martha, knotting cotton rags into the child's hair – *who's Mrs. Simpson,* the child asks, asleep before the answer

and she wakes to the sound of clogs in the cobbled yard and the Atco on the lawn leaving dark stripes in the dew, and this is the day, the day after the Jubilee fête, that Harold's dad goes into the pen and is gored by Threlkeld's black bull

so the next week candles are lit in St.Joseph's, the red lamp shines over the tabernacle, *Introibo ad altare Dei, I will go unto the altar of God,* says Father Livsey, *Ad Deum qui laetificat juventutem meum, to God who gives joy to my youth,* say the altar-boys, but the choir sings *De profundis,* and where now is the joy? Where is it?

DOWN AMONG THE SILVERFISH

Right down there,
faces pressed to the floor,
we embraced and set up house
together, became familiar
with the geography of concrete,
its cracks and fissures,
the cement's crumbling shore,
those archipelagos of tear stains,
the midnight journeyings
of snail, slug and woodlouse,
the rustling of nameless beetles –
we shared the rasping exequies
of frogs and nightjars,
lay dreamless, sleepless
in each other's arms
throughout the owl-time
and all the ticking
death-watch hours –
there was no choice for us,
we knew our place,
that we deserved to lie,
night after night, down
among the silverfish, that
we were made for each other,
Grief and I.

THE ELUSIVE SCENT OF VIOLETS

Small revenant, how you cling
to the thin air of this empty room
trailing a skein of dust
and that frayed scarf of Indian silk
I used in binding up your jaw –
my fingers fumbling and the knot
so loose that even now you wear
this uneasy shadow of a smile –
how you reproach me for the end
of it all, for the bad dreams, so sure
we left you shut out at nights, cold
and alone, on the terrace here,
or how the bright lights hurt your eyes
and the dim lights frightened you –
such terror of the dark – for the months
you drifted on that rippling bed,
the breath fluttering in your mouth
longing to escape, and cruel epithets
of pain etched into your skin,
though it was still so soft to touch
and still smelled as sweet – even now
you keep that elusive scent of violets.

SARDINES

Her first house-party
and long frock, but now
she is stuck here in the dark,
crammed into a linen cupboard
with a man she doesn't know
who's at least forty
and he's wearing tails, plus
some sort of cummerbund
and she is praying –

Please, please, Holy Mother Mary,
let me be found by the others,
by someone, anyone else
before he does it again,
before he sticks his tongue
so far into my mouth
that I'm going to be sick –

God, but you're sweet, he says,
pushing his thighs against hers,
you smell like chrysanthemums –
with her nose jammed
into his stiff shirtfront,
all she can smell is the starch,
his tar breath, her wet taffeta
and the stinking fish-sweat.

THANKS TO YOU, CHARLIE CHESTER

Sheep's eyes, sand pies, a watch without
a spring, you can buy a pomegranate too
in the old bazaar in Cairo –

Broke as usual, we ate out
somewhere in the back streets
of Al Qahirah, the triumphant city,
bravely trying labna, koshary, leleq,
basbusa, pestered by swarms
of doe-eyed boys, clamouring
to sell us yet more food, coins, scarabs,
their sisters, the pyramids – until
we escaped them and, dodging
between the swaying waiters
with coffee trays aloft, we slipped
at last into the gloom of Shepheard's
and its weary grandeur, into
the cold welcome of its marble floors,
with no good reason that I could see
for the choice, except, perhaps,
that once, during the war,
you had jumped from its balcony –
a boasted act that, if true,
I secretly thought silly.

Mamadan, Ramadan, everything in style,
genuine, bedouin, carpets with a pile,
in the old bazaar in Cairo –

The perfect place for a first fuck,
you said, positioning me on the bed,
but to be honest with you, and no,
I didn't tell you this at the time –
being a virgin, I had no expectations –

with hindsight, neither the place
nor the act itself were all that
perfect: the bed uncomfortable
and the sex being over
almost before it began, so what
I remember most about the week –
apart from those earrings we bought
in the City of the Dead's suq al guma'a,
plus the flies, feluccas, falafel
and Fahid – is that stupid song
you sang, prancing starkers
round our room, my knickers
on your head, doing what you
swore was a sand dance, a one-man
Wilson, Keppel and Betty.

THE TORAFUGU FEAST

In the garden of number ten, Mr Hashimoto
strings out new blowfish lanterns

in the bare branches of the cherry trees
and steps back to admire his handiwork

while by the gate, Mrs Hashimoto smiles, bows
to the neighbours, whispers, *Tonight, party,*

you come, yes? Sharp six-thirty, please?
All day they salivate, anticipating

saki, seaweed, wasabi, pickled ginger,
teriyaki, how their lascivious tongues

will curl round moist sushi and fugu sashimi,
round crisp tempura prawns.

Meanwhile, in the kitchen, famous chef
Noguchi is sharpening his knives. Tonight

he will prepare *cirri*, the fugu soup for which,
after years of practice, he is licensed.

First he removes the skin, sets it aside,
next there is draining of blood, the delicate

removal of ovaries, muscles, intestines,
then finally he prays – and extracts the liver.

Nobody will remember just what time it was
when the lanterns swam free from the branches

and, baring great teeth, took to chasing prawns,
silversides and krill between the houses.

Was it before or after this that the guests became
light-headed and everyone's lips grew numb?

THE SWEET SCENT OF HAWTHORN

You say the moon too is horned
but, as I see it from this angle, she is a raised eyebrow
and perhaps we have surprised her

for the cows too seem mildly astonished,
wide-eyed at our intricacies, chewing things over,
puzzled by such ineptitude –

they circle nearer, their broad flanks
hung with castanets of dung that click, click, click
to our quickening rhythm –

there is a lot of head-tossing and heavy breathing,
something sweet and foxy in the air,
our sweat mashing with the scent of hawthorn.

HARVEST MOON

When he left her in January
she was as empty as the new moon.

In February, her veined breasts
grew tender, the nipples hardened

and stood out from their dark areolas
while the days lengthened and greened up.

By the end of April her white belly fluttered,
became streaked with blue, curving

smooth and fertile as a mushroom. Through
June, July and August she dreamed time away,

drifting about the silent house like tumbleweed,
rootless, limbs heavy, her hands

pressed to the aching hollow of her back
but on the first night in September she rose

and sailed out proudly, round and swollen
as a harvest moon, to greet her daughter.

EARLY MASS, 1944

Et Introibo ad altare Dei – rusting bicycles
lie slumped against the railings, we bend our heads
over pews of yellowing pine – that acrid hint of resin –
the cold from flagstones seeps into our knees.

Ad Deum, qui laetificat juventutem meum –
mud freezes on our shoes, we rub chilblained hands,
the iced, incense-laden air knifes into our lungs
through pinched nostrils.

Quam dilecta, tabernacula tua – someone has jammed
chrysanthemums and ivy into a tarnished vase,
the utility candles snap and stutter, weep grey tears
onto the altar-cloth, windows gape, their stained glass gone.

Vere dignum et justum est – it seems right to be
so hungry and so cold, offering Mass for those at war,
our stranger-fathers, our round-eyed brothers and sisters
gawky in caps and uniforms too big, too stiff for them.

Ite, Missa est – we throw missals and mantillas
into battered baskets, bike back to breakfast, hands
on hips or standing on the pedals, weave between potholes,
shouting insults, suddenly happy, the wind behind us.

I HAVE LOOKED ON THE FACES OF THE DEAD

They do not sleep, they are not
just in the next room,
they have not passed peacefully
on before, they are gone,
clearly and terribly,
with no comfort to be had
in them – even before
they were put in the earth
they were lost to me.

If they are anywhere, my mother,
my child, my three brothers,
my friend Nina, my lovers,
they have not let me know,
there have been no messages,
no rapping on tables

and if, occasionally, I feel
one or other of them to be
near me for a while, it is only
in much the same way
I imagine at times
to be in the presence of God,
think that I have been
somewhere before,

know what lies round
the next corner, what someone
is about to say – or that you
will telephone – and I remind
myself that scientists can give
rational explanations
for all such things
which is more than can be said
for any of the churches.

LA MATANZA
Madrid 2004

Look how the unshrouded dead
are flung between the wreckage layers
of destroyed compartments,
their somehow-unbloodied faces
strung along wires and twisted
steel. That woman there, Dante
and Hieronymus would know her
at once, head askew, the eyes'
indignant upward stare,
the surprised O of her mouth
while this one here, it seems
she lies asleep, *una bella*
durmiente, behind these metal
thorns – but think how they woke
today like us, dragging themselves
from dreams or lovers' arms,
took showers, put coffee on,
chose shoes and shirts and jeans
or frocks to wear, turned back
to wave at those who stayed behind
or laughed and blew them kisses
then ran to catch their trains.

IN THE FAMILY

A nonconformist wind comes coldly off the Broads,
cutting through reed-beds towards the house

in a swirl of husks and seed-heads. Indoors
women hover while the the men eat,

their jaws churning like tractor wheels
in mud, but the girl at the kitchen window

is silent, hemmed in by a triangulation of webs.
She leans against the sink, stares into a garden

drenched in cuckoo-spit, dreams of white shawls
and stirs the water with a tow-haired mop.

The kitchen clock edges her towards her time,
she sees the birds crowd in as she shrinks back,

hearing a thin skull crack beneath their beaks –
she cries out, tells the child she carries

of the boards that creak, the shadow on the wall
that climbs her stair, of her father's hands that twist

into her hair and thrust between her thighs –
her words spill into the air and fountain upward

as she absolves herself in gibberish.
The women smile, their pale eyes sly,

complacent. *Our Elly has the Gift of Tongues*
they say, *it's in the family.*

FIRE AND WATER

You unknot your legs, stretching them out
across the sand, a St.Elmo's fire of fine gold hair.

I refuse to discuss this with you – your words
drift seaward on a twist of Marlboro smoke.

A butterfly kites out across the bay,
small shadow between two stabbing gulls.

I take to the water but the beach falls away
and the undertow drags me down.

My hands plead, clutch at silica grains, shells,
steamer glass, driftwood, las piedras del Santa Maria.

As I go under, a baptismal wind anoints me
with fine spray, puts salt upon my tongue,

breathes into my nostrils the sour-sweet stench
of putrefaction from where, behind me on the shore,

the sand-lilies thrust naked, thin and white
as neglected children. Coming up for the third

time, I reach out to you, but your eyes glass over,
are burning discs of silver, my mouth silts up with ash.

MISS BURNTHWAITE'S GAZEBO

And this is where she worked – oh, I'm so glad, it is charming, isn't it? Supposedly designed by Lutyens, a very dear friend, though sadly, I feel, he never quite gave her the credit she deserved. Not that it bothered her, dear me no, she knew what she did best and that was enough.

No, just as it was – nothing has been changed here since she passed over, I see to that. These are her spectacles, we had a little joke about them. Madame Pince-nez I called her – while I was always Pug to her. Do forgive me, just a touch of hay fever! Yes – this is her favourite hat, rather battered, I fear but she wore it every day, wet or dry – and these are her plans, plant lists and labels. Miss Burnthwaite was most particular about labelling. *No backsliding, Pug,* she'd say, *no slacking there, I want all these Nivalis sorted out by sundown.* A bit of a Tartar? Well, some people thought so, but it was just her manner, more bark than bite, and underneath, really the kindest of hearts – it's not as if she knew about my rheumatism.

Over here, everybody! If you look through this window – goodness me, a cobweb – what would she have said – you can just see the Hosta bed and the Hazel Walk, planted by both of us in about nineteen-twenty, yes, alternate groupings of green and purple Corylus, quite a sensation at the time but much copied nowadays and not always appropriately, I'm afraid, Miss Burnthwaite was awfully keen on appropriate planting. *Consult the genius loci, Puggy,* that's what she'd say – what's that? I didn't quite hear, oh, most certainly, happy times, very happy times and I count myself lucky to have been her friend – I think I may call myself that, after all those years together.

Now - if you are quite sure you've seen everything – who would like some tea? If I say so myself, my Goosenargh cakes are really rather special.

OLD JAMES GATTY CLINGS ON TO SLEEP

It is the sea, crawling over the mackerel sand,
gnawing at his door, or perhaps it is the rats
that scratch all night in the attic overhead.
He puts out a hand, feels for the painted tile
brought in Egypt, so many years ago,
his sweet grey bird of sleep
which he keeps beside the bed.

He is barely awake, James Gatty,
before the graphite sky that comes before dawn
swallows him once more – he stares down
through clear water at the dead children
twisting in the weeds – he tries to say
*I can't help yo*u, but the words won't come,
his hat has floated away, someone is shouting,
get up, get up, you've got a brain,
get up and use it.

Once again he buries his face in the soft grey folds
of his mother's dove silk tea-gown. *Lullah, lullah,*
*lullah bye-by*e, she sings, *do you want the moon*
to play with, the stars to run away with,
hush now, don't you cry – all he wants is
to stay there, for tomorrow the train comes,
it will take him back to school,
back to the mill town,
back to Paschendaele.

Stop wasting my time, his father says, *don't waste*
*your bullet*s, shouts Sergeant Trotter, *never waste*
*an erectio*n, whispers Spooner Graham
but all he wants is to rest his head
on the softly-feathered breast
of the sweet grey bird – *soucrroo,*
it sings, *soucrroo, soucrroo.*

ALLERGIES

Imagine now a shiv –
so slim, so sweetly honed,
it slips through your ribs
and upwards to the heart
as you smile on
till the pink froth
round your lying mouth
shows that I've hit home.

Or picture this – soft music,
candlelight, good wine,
perhaps Lynch Bages –
for me, an omelette
au fines herbes,
while for you, risotto
of wild mushrooms
with porcini, chanterelle –
and amanita – but who can say
how that got there?

At the inquest, of course,
I'll tell them everything –
of your culinary skills,
your boasted expertise
with the rarer fungi,
the low-carbohydrate
diet I'm on, and all my
well-documented allergies.

LETTER FROM RATHCOURSEY

Sweetheart, I write to tell you how the sun
has glazed the distant stubble fields with light
and that the old zinc bucket which you filled
with weeds still squats upon the grey stone steps
before the painted door. What would you call
that colour? Dusty, or slate, or maybe
breast-of-dove? Rathcoursey blue will have
to serve for now. Then also, you should know,
ten Tortoiseshells, a Cabbage White and two
Red Admirals have spread their wings upon
the purple buddleia which grows beside
our wind-raked washing line and, yes, the wren
still flits among the fennel's rattling seeds
but more than this, the house and I, the ducks,
geese, sun, butterflies and wren –
even the dented bucket – all long for your
return. Ridiculous, you'll say, but no less true
for that. Time creeps, the bread is proved,
come back, come back, we wait for you,
the Aga kettle sings, the whiskey's poured.

ON MY BIRTHDAY, I TRAVEL IN EXPECTATION

Meet me under the warthog, you said –
but my plane is late, it spirals down
towards Kennedy as the turquoise eyes
of countless swimming pools
stare up at me, the two guys
at immigration have cold-sores,
and the yellow cab takes it slow
on the ride in. Fourth of July,
not yet dark, but already thousands
cluster along the East River
while kids who look too young to drive
lean out of beat-up Chevys,
waving beer cans, anticipating
the premature eruption of rockets.
By the time we reach West 44th
I know more about the driver's wife
than I care to, a poster admonishes
Honey, if he don't wear a condom,
he ain't gettin' any. It's three hours
since my e.t.a, the light has vanished,
a porter unlocks the door, lets me in
to a pillared hall, calls your room.
Everything is closed, even the Late-Nite
Sushi is barred to us; side by side
we wait for the elevator in silence,
the stuffed head of the warthog
shot by a Roosevelt hangs on the wall
above us, the look on his face
somehow familiar. A window lights up
in the offices across the street,
there's a cough from the next room,
the air-conditioning has failed –
tired, thirsty, hungry, we make do
with peanuts and cola from the mini-bar –
it becomes clear that sex is off –
now I long for Smirnoff, root beer,

chowder, oyster-crackers, dough-balls,
buffalo-wings, biscuits-and-gravy,
meat-loaf, scrapple, stuffed quahogs,
apple pie, brownies, a Hershey bar,
a BLT - tomorrow I'll call Maja, together
we'll sit on those steps outside the Met,
buy hot dogs, lick the mustard.

PAY DAY

The last day of May – overnight
the garden has opened out,

firethorns drip cream
along the boundary fence,

poppies rise up
from glaucous leaves,

spread split red skirts,
reveal their black centres,

their secret places, silk filaments,
the puckered green of their sex,

everywhere such generosity –
and you, love, closed tight, tight

as a miser's tight fist on pay day,
you, too, now open yourself to me.

DINNER IN LA CORUÑA

Old hands at this, we order *percebes, minchas,*
cigales, cabrachos and *lamprejas* – but this
does not please our waiter who insists
we use the English version of the menu
from which he warmly recommends
Scrambles of Tender Garlics, Wide Open
Olives, A Sort of Fish, Weak Rice
with Snips of Lobster, Toast of Turnip Greens
with Hat of St. Simon and Comb of Pork,
A Small Bowl of Rice with Tasty, Tasty Bacon,
and – with a final flourish, he conjures up for us
Today's Specials – Galician Back-of-the-Knee
or Warm Escalabola with Cod's Tears –
in a last bid for independence, we settle
for A Crispy of King Prawns, followed by
Pale Ice-Cream with Saucy Oranges and Scum.

MALLARD

Eight mallard in the park,
seven drakes
hassling the duck.
Wisely she keeps
away from the water,
knowing that drowning
often follows a fuck.

POT LUCK

If she hadn't met
Lavinia in Ken High
and if Lavinia hadn't asked her
to share a flat in Chelsea
with Claire and Thomasina
and if Claire's brother Roger
just out of Sandhurst
hadn't brought his best friend
Rupert Pratt-Mather
back for supper one night
she might never have lived
unhappily ever after.

TEMPTATION

I met the Devil walking out today.
He asked for company along his way.

No Sir, I said, for my mother told me
that those who keep the Devil's company

soon find themselves upon the path to Hell.
The Devil laughed and said he knew her well.

HAPPY HOUR AT THE PIG AND POLECAT

Crammed in, as Jason says,
like ferrets in a posing-pouch,
you couldn't push a sausage-stick
between us, and old Nick,
that's our landlord,
a terrific bloke,
the twenty-stone bastard,
and just back,
from his usual trip
in Thailand – God,
he makes us laugh,
you should hear the one
about these two girls,
he swears they're no more
than twelve or thirteen
if they're a day, but a pair
of real little goers
and gagging for it
apparently,
well, between them
they give him the full works
a right going over,
a Bangkok sandwich
he called it, makes you sweat
even to think of it –
so next year
we'll be going with him –
yeah, the Pub outing –
well wicked.

TAPAS

Despite everything you're such an optimist
while I, on the other hand,
expect the worst and usually find it.

Tonight, for instance, the calamares
that you ordered are quite perfect
while my patatas bravas have lost heart

but I eat them, noting that the last two years
have turned your hair to grey
and how, surprisingly, it suits you

and how too, in the murky candlelight
of this overpriced wine-bar,
your eyes are quick and blue as garfish

and it's kind of you to ask, but there have been,
after all, more than twenty-two years
of occasional meetings and overseas calls,

of wry amusement at each other's amourettes –
it is surely too late to start, and so,
though you kiss me on the lips and eyelids

in that familiar and intimate way of an old lover,
though we stand here like gobsmacked teenagers,
muchas gracias, but no.

MISREADING THE ENTRAILS

That time your bay horse went lame
and we sat in the barn
smoking Passing Clouds
and watching butterflies
swarm over the privet bush
and the poor horse resting
one pointed hoof on the ground
that way they do when it hurts them
and the shadows lengthening
in the late-afternoon hush
and I was just thinking
how I could stay there
with you almost for ever
and that you would kiss me
any time now
and it was about then
you threw away your cigarette
and I yelled at you, because of the hay
and you said OK, OK, I'm sorry –
and told me the next day
you were off to be a priest
and I laughed and punched you
because it was such a good joke –
only the way life turned out
things weren't all that funny
and so, though it's been great
to see you again
and no, the child isn't yours,
believe me, I would far rather
eat a load of your old horse's shit
than call you Father.

REUNION

After three months he returned.
It's been too long, he moaned,
twisting her arms. He sighed
over her cooking, called it sexy,
whispered that her secret blend
of garlic, chilli, lemon grass
and thyme had given the salmon
a sublimely dangerous edge,
that the bottle of Gros Plant was flirty
and for once had travelled well,
then made love to her again.
So when, perhaps by accident,
he hit playback on his answer-phone
and when, between those
chummy messages from his dentist –
something about bridgework –
from his mother, three times,
and from some breezy friends
suggesting golf, when then,
a younger voice breathed
Mon Amour, Je t'aime –
she reached out for the fish knife
then slashed down, swift and sure.

THE BEAR TRAINER

Here's your music,
a march, a polka or slow waltz,
it's all the same to them,
the grinning piss-heads.

Go on, smile back,
they'll love it.

Ah, growl, would you?
I'll learn you yet
and if honey won't do it,
stick will.

So don't think,
you shambling ragbag,
you stinking heap
of flea-bitten shoddy,
to put one over on me.

In a lifetime at this game
I've seen it all
from bigger, angrier,
hornier brutes than you,
teeth and claws
can't scare me.

What,
you don't like these hot coals?
Then dance, you bugger,
dance.

YOUR LETTER DID NOT COME TODAY

I recognised it at once –
the way it failed to make
its usual bellyflop
down onto the mat,
every unwritten
flourish and curlicue
in blue-black Stephenson's
on the absent grey weave
of Conqueror's Smooth Satin,
the faintest smear of saliva
which should have been
where, oddly enough,
a first-class stamp wasn't,
the trace of your after-shave –
spice and sandalwood,
that somehow eluded me –
and if only you had seen
how eagerly I didn't
tear open the envelope,
how easily I was seduced
by every ardent word
not found there, and how,
above all, I was entranced
with the way you'd added
those seven sweet
and non-existent kisses –

LEGACIES

And for you, my rosewood sewing-box,
she said – now it stands, polished and delicate

beside my bed, a neat sarcophagus
in this untidy room, so out of place here

that for weeks I hesitate to open it,
disturb what she last put away

but today I pluck up courage, blowing
off the dust as one who brushes softly

through layers of sand to find small artefacts
in the detritus of a tomb.

What power the everyday possessions
of the dead have to move us –

I finger an ivory spool, a needle-case,
her scissors, silver thimbles,

these twists of silk and cotton thread,
hear her singing Gershwin,

catch the soft, sad, violet scent
of Pivet's Floramie.

ON DUXON HILL

Look, Tiggs, a plover's nest –
the thumb-stick points,

dripping with mud,
marsh-marigolds and weed.

Another step would crush
these khaki eggs, four of them

lying freckled and exposed
in this fragile saucer

of dry grass. My hand held tight
in his, I'm safe, wrapped up

in the warm smell of tweed
and Gold Flake, beneath

the peewits' ever-circling wings.
He is at ease here on the hill,

well-camouflaged, a speckled shape
in brown plus-fours, his anger

drained away, a grizzled ram,
moving surely now

through the beloved landscape,
an old tup with his lamb.

THE FUNERAL AT LANGHO

Hung-over, trying to remember
once-familiar hymns,
we followed the undertaker's men
as they shouldered your coffin
out into November, out into the wind
which flailed down from the fells,
hurling rooks across the sky,
limp mourning rags,
their high, cracked threnody
drowning out the priest.

For months after, I dreamt of this,
the opening of the vault,
being unable to stop it,
watching you go alone
in the brass-trimmed box
down into that black space
but now I dream we're home
again, you at the kitchen table
in your thick white dressing-gown,
your face turned away,

Polar Bear Daddy back, still angry
with me, and I plead, *It's not my fault.*

THE APPLE BOUGH

Last night a bough fell
from our old apple tree
and now, like some
heraldic beast of prey,
lies couchant in the grass
over by the blue gate
that leads into the park.

The children claimed it,
all day they have ridden
its bucking branches
and fought within its twigs,
their skin smeared
by the ancient lichen
silvering its bark.

Now, with its green leaves
and little yellow apples
twined into their hair
they are out there still,
chasing and calling
to each other,
long, long after dark.

A QUESTION OF GREEN PARAKEETS

There they go, the green parakeets –
that sudden flash against the blue,
that vapour trail of squawks –
Como las mujeres chafarderas,
Antonio says, and his wife, Maria,
laughs, lashing out at him
with the wooden olive-spoon –
he ducks, of course – but enough
of this, what concerns me is
the reality of now, or should I say
the unreality, you decide – and if
time is circular as you maintain,
have the parakeets just arrived
in this particular plaça, at noon
precisely, or just left, merely
to return next year, next century,
next millennium or when?
And not only the parakeets,
but you and I, Antonio, our table,
Maria, the raised olive-spoon –
OK, think of it another way,
remember how, in London,
all those years ago, we'd party
on the Circle Line, filling our glasses
in that pub there used to be –
what was its name – on the platform
at Sloane Square, everyone air-kissing,
drinking gin and orangeade
or Moroccan wine, while the train
carried us round, and back to where
we'd started from, how we'd refill
our flasks before careering on – it
worries me – are we still circling there,
the then held with the now
and today's parakeets in some
space-time continuum? God only knows,
I'm no philosopher, no physicist,

forget I asked – those bloody birds,
they're back again – look, another
glass of txacoli, my friend, or try
one of these, Maria's poverones,
she swears they're freshly made.